all the small poems

all the small poems

by Valerie Worth
pictures by Natalie Babbitt

A Sunburst Book

Michael di Capua Books

Farrar, Straus and Giroux

For George, with love

small poems

more small poems

still more small poems

small poems again

small poems

porches

On the front porch
Chairs sit still;

The table will receive
Summer drinks;

They wait, arranged,
Strange and polite.

On the back porch
Garden tools spill;

An empty basket
Leans to one side;

The watering can
Rusts among friends.

COW

The cow
Coming
Across the grass
Moves
Like a mountain
Toward us;
Her hipbones
Jut
Like sharp
Peaks
Of stone,
Her hoofs
Thump
Like dropped
Rocks:
Almost
Too late
She stops.

zinnias

Zinnias, stout and stiff,
Stand no nonsense: their colors
Stare, their leaves
Grow straight out, their petals
Jut like clipped cardboard,
Round, in neat flat rings.

Even cut and bunched,
Arranged to please us
In the house, in water, they
Will hardly wilt—I know
Someone like zinnias; I wish
I were like zinnias.

chairs

Chairs
Seem
To
Sit
Down
On
Themselves, almost as if
They were people,
Some fat, some thin;
Settled comfortably
On their own seats,
Some even stretch out their arms
To
Rest.

sun

The sun
Is a leaping fire
Too hot
To go near,

But it will still
Lie down
In warm yellow squares
On the floor

Like a flat
Quilt, where
The cat can curl
And purr.

coins

Coins are pleasant
To the hand:

Neat circles, smooth,
A little heavy.

They feel as if
They are worth something.

aquarium

Goldfish
Flash
Gold and silver scales;
They flick and slip away
Under green weed—
But round brown snails
Stick
To the glass
And stay.

pig

The pig is bigger
Than we had thought
And not so pink,
Fringed with white
Hairs that look
Gray, because while
They say a pig is clean,
It is not always; still,
We like this huge, cheerful,
Rich, soft-bellied beast—
It wants to be comfortable,
And does not care much
How the thing is managed.

jewels

In words, in books,
Jewels blaze and stream
Out of heaped chests
Or soft, spilled bags:
Diamonds, sharp stars,
Polished emerald tears,
Amethysts, rubies, opals
Spreading fire-surfaced pools,
Pearls falling down
In foam-ropes, sparks
Of topaz and sapphire strewn
Over a dark cave-floor—
How dim, then, the ring
Worn on the finger,
With one set stone.

tractor

The tractor rests
In the shed,
Dead or asleep,

But with high
Hind wheels
Held so still

We know
It is only waiting,
Ready to leap—

Like a heavy
Brown
Grasshopper.

grass

Grass on the lawn
Says nothing:
Clipped, empty,
Quiet.

Grass in the fields
Whistles, slides,
Casts up a foam
Of seeds,

Tangles itself
With leaves: hides
Whole rustling schools
Of mice.

dog

Under a maple tree
The dog lies down,
Lolls his limp
Tongue, yawns,
Rests his long chin
Carefully between
Front paws;
Looks up, alert;
Chops, with heavy
Jaws, at a slow fly,
Blinks, rolls
On his side,
Sighs, closes
His eyes: sleeps
All afternoon
In his loose skin.

raw carrots

Raw carrots taste
Cool and hard,
Like some crisp metal.

Horses are
Fond of them,
Crunching up

The red gold
With much wet
Juice and noise.

Carrots must taste
To horses
As they do to us.

marbles

Marbles picked up
Heavy by the handful
And held, weighed,
Hard, glossy,
Glassy, cold,
Then poured clicking,
Water-smooth, back
To their bag, seem
Treasure: round jewels,
Slithering gold.

clock

This clock
Has stopped,
Some gear
Or spring
Gone wrong—
Too tight,
Or cracked,
Or choked
With dust;
A year
Has passed
Since last
It said
Ting ting
Or tick
Or tock.
Poor
Clock.

duck

When the neat white
Duck walks like a toy
Out of the water
On yellow rubber-skinned feet,

And speaks wet sounds,
Hardly opening
His round-tipped wooden
Yellow-painted beak,

And wags his tail,
Flicking the last
Glass water-drops
From his flat china back,

Then we would like
To pick him up, take
Him home with us, put him
Away, on a shelf, to keep.

daisies

Where the dusty lane
Wound dull and plain
Among blind weeds,
Today daisies
Have opened a petal-
Decorated way
For us to walk;
The two fluttering, white-
Fringed, golden-eyed banks
Seem wide celebrations—
As if earth were glad
To see us passing here.

pie

After the yellow-white
Pie dough is rolled out
Flat, and picked up
Drooping like a round
Velvet mat, fitted gently
Into the dish, and piled
With sliced, sugared,
Yellow-white apples,
Covered with still another
Soft dough-blanket,
The whole thing trimmed
And tucked in tight, then
It is all so neat, so
Thick and filled and fat,
That we could happily
Eat it up, even
Before it is cooked.

frog

The spotted frog
Sits quite still
On a wet stone;

He is green
With a luster
Of water on his skin;

His back is mossy
With spots, and green
Like moss on a stone;

His gold-circled eyes
Stare hard
Like bright metal rings;

When he leaps
He is like a stone
Thrown into the pond;

Water rings spread
After him, bright circles
Of green, circles of gold.

pebbles

Pebbles belong to no one
Until you pick them up—
Then they are yours.

But which, of all the world's
Mountains of little broken stones,
Will you choose to keep?

The smooth black, the white,
The rough gray with sparks
Shining in its cracks?

Somewhere the best pebble must
Lie hidden, meant for you
If you can find it.

hollyhocks

Hollyhocks stand in clumps
By the doors of old cottages.

Even when one springs alone,
Lost, in an uncut field,

It builds beside it the cottage,
The garden, the old woman, the beehive.

cat

The spotted cat hops
Up to a white radiator-cover
As warm as summer, and there,

Between pots of green leaves growing,
By a window of cold panes showing
Silver of snow thin across the grass,

She settles slight neat muscles
Smoothly down within
Her comfortable fur,

Slips in the ends, front paws,
Tail, until she is readied,
Arranged, shaped for sleep.

fence

The old fence
Has fallen down,
A pile of gray
Rails resting
In the grass.

Where are all
The cows now,
That leaned
Hard there,
Hoping to get out?

Have they pushed
Through, and walked
Down the road,
Past all fences
Forever?

crickets

Crickets
Talk
In the tall
Grass
All
Late summer
Long.
When
Summer
Is gone,
The dry
Grass
Whispers
Alone.

more small poems

magnifying glass

Small grains
In a stone
Grow edges
That twinkle;

The smooth
Moth's wing
Sprouts feathers
Like shingles;

My thumb
Is wrapped
In rich
Satin wrinkles.

kitten

The black kitten,
Arched stiff,
Dances sidewise
From behind
The chair, leaps,
Tears away with
Ears back, spins,
Lands crouched
Flat on the floor,
Sighting something
At nose level,

Her eyes round
As oranges, her
Hind legs marking
Time: then she
Pounces, cactus-
Clawed, upon
A strayed
Strand of fluff:
Can anyone
Believe that she
Doesn't ask us
To laugh?

safety pin

Closed, it sleeps
On its side
Quietly,
The silver
Image
Of some
Small fish;

Opened, it snaps
Its tail out
Like a thin
Shrimp, and looks
At the sharp
Point with a
Surprised eye.

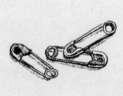

earthworms

Garden soil,
Spaded up,
Gleams with
Gravel-glints,
Mica-sparks, and
Bright wet
Glimpses of
Earthworms
Stirring beneath:

Put on the palm,
Still rough
With crumbs,
They roll and
Glisten in the sun
As fresh
As new rubies
Dug out of
Deepest earth

lawnmower

The lawnmower
Grinds its teeth
Over the grass,
Spitting out a thick
Green spray;

Its head is too full
Of iron and oil
To know
What it throws
Away:

The lawn's whole
Crop of chopped
Soft,
Delicious
Green hay.

sparrow

Nothing is less
Rare than
One dust-
Colored sparrow
In a driveway
Minding her own
Matters, pottering
Carelessly, finding
Seeds in the tire-
Flattened weeds:

But because
She can dare
To let us watch her
There, when all
The stately robins
Have fled
Scolding into
The air, she
Is as good a bird
As anyone needs.

magnet

This small
Flat horseshoe
Is sold for
A toy: we are
Told that it
Will pick up pins
And it does, time
After time; later
It lies about,
Getting its red
Paint chipped, being
Offered pins less
Often, until at
Last we leave it
Alone: then

It leads its own
Life, trading
Secrets with
The North Pole,
Reading
Invisible messages
From the sun.

lions

Bars, wire,
Glass, and rails, and
Even two men
Washing down
The concrete cells
Toward gutter tiles
Where the water
Flows away,

Cannot keep
From the aisles
The harsh gold
Smell of lions,
Luckily: otherwise
They could be heavy
Puppets of plush-
Covered clay.

acorn

An acorn
Fits perfectly
Into its shingled
Cup, with a stick
Attached
At the top,

Its polished
Nut curves
In the shape
Of a drop, drawn
Down to a thorn
At the tip,

And its heart
Holds folded
Thick white fat
From which
A marvelous
Tree grows up:

I think no better
Invention or
Mechanical trick
Could ever
Be bought
In a shop.

caterpillar

The feet of the
Caterpillar
Do not patter
As he passes
Like the clever
Quick paws
Of the squirrel,
But they ripple,
Stepping one pair
After another
And another,
And they travel
With his whole
Long caravan
Of bristles
Down the brown
Twig, to a
Greener midsummer
Dinner.

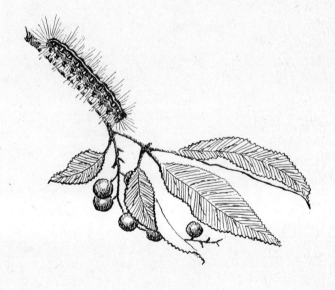

fireworks

First
A far thud,
Then the rocket
Climbs the air,
A dull red flare,
To hang, a moment,
Invisible, before
Its shut black shell cracks
And claps against the ears,
Breaks and billows into bloom,
Spilling down clear green sparks, gold spears,
Silent sliding silver waterfalls and stars.

flamingo

The
Flamingo
Lingers
A
Long
Time
Over
One
Pink
Leg;

Later
He
Ponders
Upon
The
Other
For
A
While
Instead.

hose

The hose
Can squeeze
Water to
A silver rod
That digs
Hard holes
In the mud,

Or, muzzled
Tighter by
The nozzle,
Can rain
Chill diamond
Chains
Across the yard,

Or, fanned
Out fine,
Can hang
A silk
Rainbow
Halo
Over soft fog.

mosquito

There is more
To a mosquito
Than her sting
Or the way she sings
In the ear:

There are her wings
As clear
As windows,
There are the sleek
Velvets on her back;

She bends six
Slender knees,
And her eye, that
Sees the swatter,
Glitters.

shoes

Which to prefer?
Hard leather heels,
Their blocks carved
Thick, like rocks,
Clacked down
Waxed wood stairs,

Or the pale soles
Of sneakers,
Worn smooth, soft
As mushroom caps,
Supple upon warm
Summer pavements?

sea lions

The satin sea lions
Nudge each other
Toward the edge
Of the pool until
They fall like
Soft boulders
Into the water,
Sink down, slide
In swift circles,
Twist together
And apart, rise again
Snorting, climb
Up slapping
Their flippers on
The wet cement:
Someone said
That in all the zoo
Only the sea lions
Seem happy.

sidewalks

Sidewalks wear out;
Some sunk squares,
Winter-cracked,
Even break:
Then their chunks
Tip up
To trip old women,
Scrape the bare
Big toe, stop
Skates that rolled
Rits, rits, before,
And slow them
To step
Dit dit dit around.

crab

The dead crab
Lies still,
Limp on dry sand,

All strength to crawl
Gone from his
Hard shell—

But he keeps a shape
Of old anger
Curved along his claws.

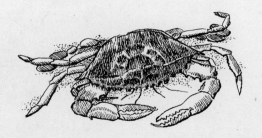

weeds

In the rough places,
Along concrete curbs,
Up railroad banks,
Next to brick buildings,
Weeds will grow;
And no one cares
If they live there,
Year after year:
Quietly attending
To roots, stalks,
Or even, above
Dusty leaves, a few
Dim stars of flowers.

haunted house

Its echoes,
Its aching stairs,
Its doors gone stiff
At the hinges,

Remind us of its
Owners, who
Grew old, who
Died, but

Who are still
Here: leaning
In the closet like
That curtain rod,

Sleeping on the cellar
Shelf like this
Empty
Jelly jar.

toad

When the flowers
Turned clever, and
Earned wide
Tender red petals
For themselves,

When the birds
Learned about feathers,
Spread green tails,
Grew cockades
On their heads,

The toad said:
Someone has got
To remember
The mud, and
I'm not proud.

pumpkin

After its lid
Is cut, the slick
Seeds and stuck
Wet strings
Scooped out,
Walls scraped
Dry and white,
Face carved, candle
Fixed and lit,

Light creeps
Into the thick
Rind: giving
That dead orange
Vegetable skull
Warm skin, making
A live head
To hold its
Sharp gold grin.

christmas lights

Bulbs strung along
Our porch roof
Pour clear
Colors through the
Cold black air;

But our neighbors
Have a spruce, like
A huge shadow,
Full of deep blue
Mysterious stars.

dinosaurs

Dinosaurs
Do not count,
Because
They are all
Dead:

None of us
Saw them, dogs
Do not even
Know that
They were there—

But they
Still walk
About heavily
In everybody's
Head.

soap bubble

The soap bubble's
Great soft sphere
Bends out of shape
On the air,
Leans, rounds again,
Rises, shivering, heavy,
A planet revolving
Hollow and clear,
Mapped with
Rainbows, streaming,
Curled: seeming
A world too splendid
To snap, dribble,
And disappear.

still more small poems

door

My grandmother's
Glass front door
Held a fancy pattern
Of panes, their
Heavy edges cut
On a slant: when
Sun shone through,
They scattered
Some eighty little
Flakes of rainbows
Into the room,
Walking the walls,
Glowing like fallen
Flowers on the floor;
Why don't they
Make front doors that
Way any more?

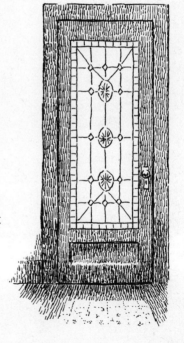

kite

The kite, kept
Indoors, wears
Dead paper
On tight-
Boned wood,
Pulls at the tied
Cord only
By its weight—

But held
To the wind,
It is another thing,
Turned strong,
Struck alive,
Wild to be torn
Away from the hand
Into high air:

Where it rides
Alone,
Glad,
A small, clear
Wing, having
Nothing at all
To do
With string.

turtle

The turtle
Does little
But sleep
On a stone,
Alone
In his glass
Bowl.

Is he bored
By it all?
Does he hope
Something
Will happen,
After a hundred
Naps?

Or is it enough
To wake
Quietly,
Shawled
In the shade
Of his
Shell?

compass

According to
The compass,
Wherever you happen
To stand,

North, south,
East and west,
Meet in the palm
Of your hand.

bell

By flat tink
Of tin, or thin
Copper tong,
Brass clang,
Bronze bong,

The bell gives
Metal a tongue—
To sing
In one sound
Its whole song.

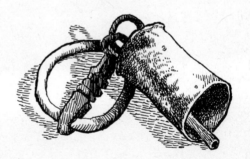

pigeons

The pigeon shed
Is hot, and smells
Of dust and corn;

Pigeon-voices
Bubble, wings scuffle
Above our heads;

We are allowed
To touch the throats
Of the young squabs:

They sink and shift
Like beanbags, heavy
With grain, and warm.

honeycomb

Sealed wax cells
Dull the honey's gold
And hold it stiff and still.

The bees build well,
But the hidden honey
Only waits to spill—

To glitter out free,
And spread itself everywhere,
The way honey will.

rags

Stuffed away into
An old pillowcase,

Dragged forth again
In crumpled clods,

Torn to wash windows
Or tie up tomato plants,

Thrown out at last—
Poor sad gray wads

That once were faithful
Flannel pajamas,

Favorite pink-
Flowered underpants.

barefoot

After that tight
Choke of sock
And blunt
Weight of shoe,

The foot can feel
Clover's green
Skin
Growing,

And the fine
Invisible
Teeth
Of gentle grass,

And the cool
Breath
Of the earth
Beneath.

mushroom

The mushroom pushes
Its soft skull
Up through the soil,

Spreads its frail
Ribs into full
Pale bloom,

And floats,
A dim ghost,
Above the tomb

Where an oak's
Old dust lies
Flourishing still.

pail

A new pail,
Straight, tight,
Brushed to a cold
Silver shine,

Soon learns
Other ways:
Once filled with
Oats or ashes,

Grayed by rain,
Its handle
Bent, its
Bottom dented,

Grown peaceful
And plain,
It becomes
A real pail.

horse

In the stall's gloom,
His back, curved
Like a high sofa,
Turns on unseen
Legs, looms closer,
Until his long
Head forms above
The door, his face
Of thin silk over
Bone: to be stroked
Carefully, like
Fine upholstery
On a hard chair.

back yard

Sun in the back yard
Grows lazy,

Dozing on the porch steps
All morning,

Getting up and nosing
About corners,

Gazing into an empty
Flowerpot,

Later easing over the grass
For a nap,

Unless
Someone hangs out the wash—

Which changes
Everything to a rush and a clap

Of wet
Cloth, and fresh wind

And sun
Wide awake in the white sheets.

rosebush

In summer it
Blooms out fat
And sweet as milk;

In winter it
Thins to a bitter
Tangle of bones;

And who can say
Which is the
True rosebush?

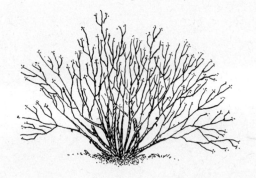

slug

The slug
Slides sly
By night,

To nibble
The new
Green shoot,

To riddle
The weak
White root—

Hated
By all
But the moon,

Who smiles
On his scenes
Of crime,

And silvers
His trails
Of slime.

rocks

They say, No
Life on the moon,
Not much, if
Any, on Mars—

But I say,
See those
Rocks: how
They stand up

Shapely against
The dust, in
Their subtle
Limbs and skins,

Showing a
Live mineral
Cleverness, just
Like rocks here.

cat bath

In the midst
Of grooming
Her inner
Thigh,

Her leg
Locked
High at
Her back,

She looks
Up: with
A pink
Crescent

Tongue
Left
Between lip
And lip.

tom

Old Tom
Comes along
The room
In steps
Laid down
Like cards,
Slow-paced
But firm,
All former
Temptations
Too humdrum
To turn
Him from
His goal:
His bowl.

roadside

Beside the road,
Narrow strips of
Field still run,
Full of pale
Grass, thin scrub,
Scrap and rust
Of things
Cast away—
A dead glove,
Empty bottle-skulls,
A shivering spirit
Of lost cellophane.

mice

Mice
Find places
In places,

A dark
Hall behind
The hall,

Odd rooms
That other
Rooms hide:

A world
Inside
The wide world,

And space enough,
Even in
Small spaces.

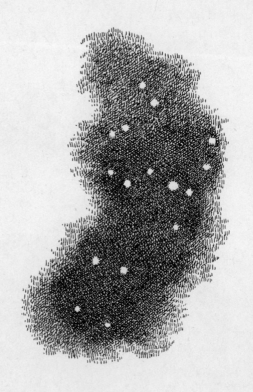

stars

While we
Know they are
Enormous suns,
Gold lashing
Fire-oceans,
Seas of heavy
Silver flame,

They look as
Though they could
Be swept
Down, and heaped,
Cold crystal
Sparks, in one
Cupped palm.

egg

Somehow the hen,
Herself all quirk
And freak and whim,

Manages to make
This egg, as pure
And calm as stone:

All for the sake
Of a silly chick,
Another squawking hen.

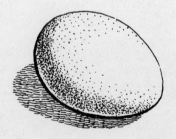

sweets

Here
Is a list
Of likely
Words
To taste:

Peppermint,
Cinnamon,
Strawberry,
Licorice,
Lime:

Strange
How they manage
To flavor
The paper
Page.

garbage

The stained,
Sour-scented
Bucket tips out
Hammered-gold
Orange rind,

Eggshell ivory,
Garnet coffee-
Grounds, pearl
Wand of bared
Chicken bone:

Worked back soon
To still more
Curious jewelry
Of chemical
And molecule.

snow

Gardens, fields,
The far hills,
Lie deathly
With white winter,

Wide drifts
And heavy deeps
Made only of
Each snowflake fallen,

Like these many
Still falling, these
Few still alive
On my sleeve—

None anywhere
Ever like
This one, this
Very one.

small poems again

amoeba

Never wondering
What shape to take,
But with a
Slow shrug
Making a start
In any direction,
And then following,
Flowing wholeheartedly
Into the fluid
Mold of the moment.

jacks

The way
Jacks nest
Together in
The hand,

Or cupped
Between
Two palms,
Jingled up

And thrown,
Land in a
Loose starry
Cluster,

Seems luxury
Enough,
Without the
Further bliss

Of their
Slender
Iridescent
Luster.

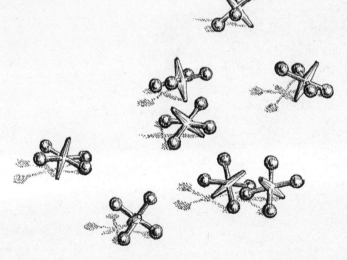

anteater

Imagine overturning
The teeming anthill
Without a qualm,
Calmly sweeping
Up its angry
Inhabitants on a
Long sticky tongue,
And swallowing the
Lot with relish—
As if those
Beady little bodies
Made just so many
Mouthfuls of red
Or black caviar.

frost

How does
The plain
Transparency
Of water

Sprout these
Lacy fronds
And plumes
And tendrils?

And where,
Before window-
Panes, did
They root

Their lush
Crystal forests,
Their cold
Silver jungles?

beetle

As in old
Mummy-times,
The scarab
Beetle keeps
Its precious
Innards
Packed in
A lacquered
Coffer of
Curious
Compartments.

robins

Look how
Last year's
Leaves, faded
So gray
And brown,

Blunder
Along
Like flimsy
Flightless
Birds,

Stumbling
Beak over
Tail
Before
The wind.

But no,
Wait:
Today
They right
Themselves,

And turn
To the
Stout slate
And ruddy
Rust

Of robins,
Running
On steady
Stems across
The ground.

kaleidoscope

Only a litter
Of bright bits,
Tipped and tumbled
Over each other
Until they huddle
Untidily all
In one corner,

Where their
Reflections wake
And break into
Crystals, petals,
Stars: only
The tricks of
Mirrors, but

Still miracles,
Like snowflakes
Shaken from jumbled
Clouds, or earth's
Rough muddle
Jostled to
Jewels and flowers.

tiger

The tiger
Has swallowed
A black sun,

In his cold
Cage he
Carries it still:

Black flames
Flicker through
His fur,

Black rays roar
From the centers
Of his eyes.

mantis

Bowing
Such lean
And monklike
Shoulders,

Robed in
Such leafily
Meek
Array,

Folding
The wrists,
And treading
So slowly,

Can it
Really be
Wholly
Holy,

Pretending
To pray,
While intending
To prey?

seashell

My father's mother
Picked up the shell
And turned it about
In her hand that was
Crinkled, glossy and
Twined with veins,
The fingers rumpled
Into soft roses
At the knuckles, and
She said, "Why did
That little creature
Take so much trouble
To be beautiful?"

asparagus

Like a nest
Of snakes
Awakened, craning
Long-necked

Out of the
Ground: to stand
With sharp
Scaly heads

Alert, tasting
The air,
Taking the sun,
Looking around.

telephone poles

Close by,
They're stolid
Stumps, sweating
Black creosote,
Scarred with
Bolts and tin
Numbers, clumsy
Old dolts
Of lumber;

But wandering
Away, they
Lean into
The cloud's
Drift, the
Swallow's slant,
The graceful
Influence of
Grass; and

Lifting up
Their long
Electric lines,
They hand
Them on
And on, in
Gestures of
Exquisite
Gossamer.

starfish

Spined
With sparks,
Limbed
With flames,

Climbing
The dark
To cling
And shine

Until the
Slow tide
Turns
Again:

Not even
Knowing
What stars
Are,

But
Even so,
The
Same.

crows

When the high
Snows lie worn
To rags along
The muddy furrows,

And the frozen
Sky frays, drooping
Gray and sodden
To the ground,

The sleek crows
Appear, flying
Low across the
Threadbare meadow

To jeer at
Winter's ruin
With their jubilant
Thaw, thaw, thaw!

fleas

Roaming these
Furry prairies,
Daring every so
Often to stop
And sink a well
In the soft pink
Soil, hoping
To draw up a
Hasty drop, and
Drink, and survive,

There's always
The threat of those
Inexplicable storms,
When over the hairy
Horizon rages
A terrible paw:
Descending to
Rend the ground,
While we scramble
Away for our lives.

coat hangers

Open the closet
And there they
Wait, in a
Trim obedient row;

Stirred by the
Air, they only
Touch wires with
A vacant jangle;

But try to
Remove just one,
And they suddenly.
Clash and cling,

And fling them-
Selves to the
Floor in an
Inextricable tangle.

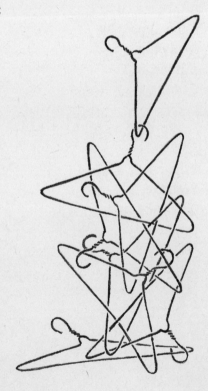

dandelion

Out of
Green space,
A sun:
Bright for
A day, burning
Away to
A husk, a
Cratered moon:

Burst
In a week
To dust:
Seeding
The infinite
Lawn with
Its starry
Smithereens.

heron

Only
Fools
Pursue
Their
Prey.

Mine
Comes to
Me, while
I stand and
Reflect:

Quick silver
Visions
Swimming into
My glassy
Reverie,

Seized
By a mere
Nod of
My wise
Beak.

library

No need even
To take out
A book: only
Go inside
And savor
The heady
Dry breath of
Ink and paper,
Or stand and
Listen to the
Silent twitter
Of a billion
Tiny busy
Black words.

octopus

Marvel at the
Awful many-armed
Sea-god Octopus,
And the coiled
Elbows of his eager
Eightfold embrace;

Yet also at his
Tapered tender
Fingertips, ferrying
Their great brow
Along the sea floor
In solitary grace.

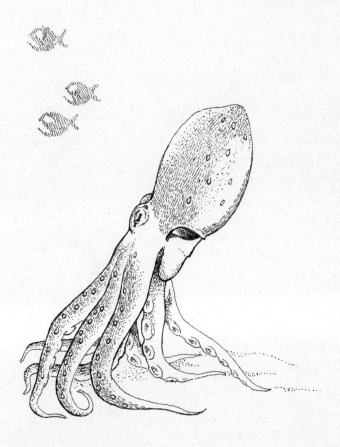

skunk

Sometimes, around
Moonrise, a wraith
Drifts in through
The open window:
A vague cold taint
Of rank weeds
And phosphorescent
Mold, a hint
Of obscure dank
Root hollows and
Mist-woven paths,
Pale toadstools and
Dark-reveling worms:
As the skunk walks
By, half vapor, half
Shade, diffusing
The night's uncanny
Essence and atmosphere.

water lily

A hundred
Shallow green
Questions pressed
Upon the
Silent pool,

Before it
Answers all
With a single
Deep white
Syllable.

broom

It starts
Out so well,
Its fresh
Gold straws
Cut square,
Flared wide,

But so often
Ends otherwise,
With weary
Wan bristles
All stubbed
To one side.

giraffe

How lucky
To live
So high
Above
The body,
Breathing
At heaven's
Level,
Looking
Sun
In the eye;
While down
Below
The neck's
Precarious
Stair,
Back, belly,
And legs
Take care
Of themselves,

Hardly
Aware
Of the head's
Airy
Affairs.

flies

Flies wear
Their bones
On the outside.

Some show dead
Gray, as bones
Should seem,

But others gleam
Dark blue, or bright
Metal-green,

Or a polished
Copper, mirroring
The sun:

If all bones
Shone so, I
Wouldn't mind

Going around
In my own
Skeleton.